Leslie Korn, **PhD**, **MPH**, **LMHC**, specializes in mental health nutrition, somatic therapies and psychotherapy for PTSD, chronic illness and optimal cognition. She completed her clinical training at Harvard Medical School and her life training in the jungle of Mexico. She is the author of *Rhythms of Recovery: Trauma, Nature,* and *the Body, Nutrition Essentials for Mental Health: The Complete Guide to the Food-Mood Connection and Multicultural Counseling Workbook: Exercises, Worksheets & Games to Build Rapport with Diverse Clients.*

🍴

Everyone can benefit from these recipes and ideas; just eat, enjoy, and learn. Simply pick a n recipe to try each week. Many of the recipes are well suited to use with children and are a fu approach to learning food preparation, the joys of cooking, and good health.

The introductory cards provide foundational ideas to get you started on a path toward impr nutrition, regardless of health status.

Each color-coded section corresponds to a different category and provides a selection of re that are formulated to ensure that the food provides essential and enjoyable support for th mind and body.

Above all, this deck is meant to provide a simple, joyous approach to food as medicine for tl

—— Ψ◯Ⅰ ——

Too often my clients would say to me, "I don't have time to cook or I don't know how to cook or I am afraid it won't come out right. "

These cards are designed to remedy all of those concerns; the recipes are easy to follow and yet easy to change with your own intuitive ideas. If you like to measure, great; if you like pinches and handfuls, these recipes will still work. These are stress-less recipes in the making. Your senses will delight in their taste as your mind absorbs the healing nutrients. I hope that you and your loved ones will find pleasure, relaxation and contentment in these dishes.

Dr. *Leslie* KORN

Eat Right, Feel Right

Over 80 Recipes and Tips to Improve
Mood, Sleep, Attention & Focus

Leslie Korn, author of *Nutrition Essentials for Mental Health*

Published by:

PESI Publishing & Media

PESI, Inc.
3839 White Ave.
Eau Claire, WI 54703

Cover Design: Aubre Walther & Amy Rubenzer

Editing: Marietta Whittlesey & Jeanie Stanek

Layout: Amy Rubenzer & Aubre Walther

Proudly printed in the United States of America

ISBN: 9781683730583

PESI Publishing & Media
www.pesipublishing.com

Table of Contents

INSOMNIA **68**

ATTENTION & FOCUS **86**

Best Foods for Moods

Mood disorders can develop from chronic stress and systemic inflammation. The best food are healthy fats to lubricate and nourish the brain, green and orange vegtables to stabilize blood sugar, and blue/red fruits to reduce inflamation.

Organic Beef, Lamb, Chicken and Pinto Beans
These types of proteins are rich in amino acids which support brain function and mood stability. Pinto beans are rich in B vitamins (especially B-6), which, together with amino acids, support a healthy mood.

Eggs
Eggs are the ideal protein for brain and memory function. They are also proven to enhance growth in children and support adults with high performance activity. Eat two organic farm eggs a day.

Olive Oil, Butter (raw, unsalted) and Coconut Fat
These good fats are medicinal for the brain and mood. Coconut fat is considered a dementia preventative and is very easily digested.

Salmon or Tuna (fresh wild, wild canned)
These fish are rich in omega 3's, which help support the brain and ease pain. Eat only wild varieties.

Fermented Foods
Fermented foods support intestinal health, enhance healthy bacteria, and promote relaxing (GABA) neurotransmitters for brain health.

Sweet Potatoes and Parsnips
These healthy mood stabilizers make an ideal meal for a sweet tooth, and also reduce inflammation. Bake to bring out the flavor and top with butter and sea salt.

Blueberries and Raspberries
Buy fresh or frozen, and enjoy the blue and red antioxidants that reduce pain and help brain function.

Lemons
Just smelling a lemon increases a sense of well-being. When feeling low in energy, cut open a lemon, sniff and then squeeze the juice into a couple tablespoons of olive oil.
Add garlic and dill, and pour over fresh vegetable for a delicious snack or side dish.

Oats

One of the most important anti-anxiety foods, oats are best eaten in the evening because they are so relaxing. Add nuts and raisins, or use them in baking.

Green Tea

Green tea is rich in theanine, a relaxing amino acid. It can be served in hot or cold tea, as a concentrate, or added to smoothies to boost the mood while staying calm.

Coffee

Boosts mood and helps focus and productivity, but be careful. Too much coffee causes anxiety and insomnia. Everyone benefits from a different amount of coffee.

Beets

One of the best foods for digestion, gallbladder health, and detoxification. Steam them or grate them on top of a salad.

Basil

These green leaves are a natural anti-inflammatory and mood lifter. It grows easily in a warm kitchen window where you can pick fresh leaves. Make pesto out of fresh basil and use it to top vegetables, fish or brown rice. Some people crush basil and mix it with lard and apply it topically to a bruise.

Figs

Figs are rich in calcium, magnesium, fiber and Vitamin K. Figs, fresh and dried, should be a staple of your diet to maintain healthy blood sugar, satiety and an elevated mood.

Bitter Greens (Arugula, Dandelion, Watercress, Parsley)

Bitter greens are used to keep the liver and gallbladder healthy, which in turn is essential for reducing anger and depression.

Best Spices & Seasonings for Mental Health

Turmeric

Turmeric contains curcumin, which is a potent anti-depressant and anti-inflammatory. Depression and chronic pain often co-occur. Buy it as a rhizome at your local Indian, Mexican or Asian market, or in powder form at the local grocery. It's the main ingredient in curry and can be added to vegetables, chicken and meat. Always use freshly ground black pepper in recipes using turmeric, as it is necessary for the absorption of the curcumin. It may also be added to a smoothie.

Garlic

Garlic has many benefits for heart health, but a little known benefit is that it helps detoxify the liver and aids in the methylation process, necessary for good mental health.

Ginger

Use ginger in stir fries or add to soups. Or, try blending a small piece in your next citrus smoothie to kick your angry mood. It stimulates and cleanses the liver, which is where according to Traditional Chinese Medicine anger lives.

Sea Salt

Sea salt is rich in minerals which support adrenal function, thus making it an important addition to a stress-reduction diet. Eliminate table salt, and experiment with pink and gray salts from different shores around the world.

Best Anxiety-Decreasing Foods

Decreasing and managing anxiety is about eliminating stimulating foods and substances, increasing GABA (a neurotransmitter) precursor foods, and ensuring that there's plenty of acidifying food in your diet, like vinegars and animal protein. Among the best foods for anxiety are bananas, figs, vinegar, and oats.

Contrary to popular custom, oats are better eaten later in the day, because they are so relaxing.

Best Fats for Mental Health

Good fats are essential to mental health, and bad fats will contribute to poor mental health. The brain is mostly fat and needs plenty of fat to function. Good fats are a source of energy, satiety, and are anti-inflammatory. Bad fats clog the arteries and cause pain and inflammation, leading to depression and memory/learning problems.

It's a myth that fats (especially saturated fats) are bad for your health. That has been disproven. In fact, without saturated fats, you cannot absorb essential vitamins like A, D, E, and K. The best step you can make is to throw out all of the bad fats and bring in the good ones. Fats and greens go together. This is why putting a healthy dollop of raw butter on your steamed greens and topping it with sea salt is a perfect way to improve mood and mental stamina.

TIP: Need help digesting fats? Bitter greens like watercress, arugula, and dandelion are the best foods to eat with a high fat meal.

Always choose organic and/or cold pressed oils; otherwise they are bad fats. Limit the times you eat out because most places use bad fats. NEVER eat deep fat fried food in a restaurant. Focus on using the following fats:

Butter

The best, most nutritious and medicinal butter is raw. Butter is medicine and the brain needs cholesterol. Splurge for raw butter since your food is your medicine. The Wulzen factor, which prevents and decreases arthritis, joint stiffness, and pain, is found only in raw butter and raw cream. Butter should be used on top of grains, vegetables or proteins; make sure not to cook it at high temperatures. Do not worry about cholesterol!

Ghee

Ghee is clarified butter. It is an ideal fat for people who are lactose intolerant because all of the milk proteins have been removed. Because it has a high smoke point, you can cook with it, unlike butter, which burns.

Coconut Oil

Use coconut oil for cooking or add to smoothies and baked goods. Coconut oil is a medium chain fatty acid. It is very easily digested, considered healing for the brain, and can aid memory. You can also use it as a moisturizer by rubbing it on dry skin.

Extra Virgin Olive Oil (cold pressed)

Olive oil should be a deep green color and bought and stored only in a dark bottle or can, away from light. It is ideal for salad dressings, less so for high heats since olive oil has a low smoke point and the chlorophyll degrades in heat. It can be combined with butter and drizzled over steamed or baked vegetables.

Flax Seed Oil

Add ¼ cup of organic flax seed oil to your olive oil-based salad dressing to gain the benefits of essential fatty acids. Flax seed oil requires refrigeration. It is never heated or used in cooking.

Sesame Oil (toasted and raw)

Long revered in Ayurvedic medicine as a healing oil, sesame is very versatile. Toasted, it adds depth of flavor to vegetable stir-frys and raw, it makes a nice, light dressing.

TIP: Swishing two tablespoons of raw sesame oil in your mouth before bed (no rinsing) is an ancient Ayurvedic remedy for gum problems. Gum problems can be associated with heart disease, which in turn can be associated with dementia. So, swish that oil every night and avoid gum surgery.

Best Foods for Focus

The key to focus and attention is plenty of protein, good fats, vegetable or fruit carbohydrates and minimal starchy carbs like wheat--in that order! Most of us need energy beginning in the morning that will last all day. The very best foods to support attention, focus, and memory are: eggs, cocoa (no refined sugar!), nut butters, and apples. Small meals or snacks every 3 -4 hours will help as well. True attention is supported with gently stimulating foods, but overuse and over-stimulation can lead to exhaustion. Don't overdo these foods and herbs. This list of naturally energizing and stimulating herbs and plants can easily be incorporated into your daily diet:

Chocolate/Cocoa

Chocolate is the "Food of the Gods" for good reason: it's divine! Without sugar, it is anti-inflammatory and high in polyphenols; however, with sugar, the benefits are destroyed. Cocoa increases circulation and blood vessel growth, improves blood flow to the brain, and supports cognitive function and memory. Cocoa lifts mood and also stimulates healthy bacteria in the gut. Limit cocoa use to 1-2 cups a day and sweeten with stevia.

Licorice Root

Make a cup of tea with licorice root. It is sweet, energizing, and detoxifying. Use it when feeling tired or if coming down with a cold. Don't drink too much if you have high blood pressure.

Rhodiola

Rhodiola reduces fatigue and improves physical performance and mental focus. It helps you cope with stress and it makes a perfect afternoon "pick-me-up." Use it as a substitute for coffee since it increases dopamine and lifts mood. Too much, however, will make you jittery just like coffee.

Ginseng

This important Chinese herb is a gentle stimulant and helps to reduce stress. It improves memory, concentration, and focus. Fresh or dried ginseng root is usually boiled and made into a tea.

Schizandra

This superfood is a berry, and is sweet, salty, sour, bitter, and pungent. It enhances mood and improves the ability to memorize and learn new information. Schizandra can be found as dried berries or in supplements.

Maca

This is a root that belongs to the broccoli family and originated in the Andes. It is energizing, and increases exercise and work endurance. Maca usually comes in a powder form and can be added to smoothies for an extra boost.

Foods to Avoid

Fried Foods

While a very occasional fried food is okay, they are very difficult on the liver and gallbladder.

Fast Foods

Fast foods are often made from poor quality ingredients, and a lot of salt and sugar, which cause inflammation. Some also contain fillers and additives designed to become addictive to your taste buds.

Margarine/Canola/Safflower/Soy/Corn Oil/Fake Butters

These foods are high in trans fats and are processed with heat (instead of cold -pressed) which makes them toxic to the liver and heart. These oils are high in Omega 6 fatty acids which can generate toxins that rigidify cell walls. The human body does not easily convert Omega 6 into the essential brain fuel DHA. The brain is made up of DHA which makes brain cells "communicate" more easily.

Corn Syrup/White Sugar/Fake Maple Syrup

These sugars are extracted and concentrated from their original source, which denatures them. This makes them inflammatory in the body, contributing to pain, cancer, diabetes, and heart disease.

Artificial Sweeteners (Aspartame, Nutrasweet)

Artificial sweeteners contain chemicals called neurotoxins or excitotoxins because they over stimulate the neurons in the brain and contribute to mood changes.

Packaged Foods with "Natural Flavors" and Additives like MSG and Preservatives

See Artificial Sweeteners above.

Processed Meats and Meat from Grain-fed Animals

Animals that provide nourishment for humans should be harvested in the wild or raised humanely, and fed food appropriate for their bodies. Avoid meat from animals fed corn, grains, or other animal byproducts as they also contain GMO, antibiotics, and hormones, which affect brain development and gut health.

Foods Made with White Flour

White flour is refined with all the nutrients and vitamins extracted. This makes it act on the body like a powerful drug. If you digest wheat, use sprouted wheat, whole wheat, or non-gluten flours to enhance well-being and avoid addiction to refined foods.

Fruit that is Canned in Sugar

Fruit is best eaten raw or slightly cooked, as in baked apples or pears. Fruit that is canned in sugar raises your blood glucose, alters mood, and makes you vulnerable to the development of diabetes.

Farmed Fish

Farmed fish are fed corn, cereals, dyes, and antibiotics. They have low levels of protein and fatty acids. Never eat farmed fish. Most fish served in restaurants is farmed, so ask where the fish is from before ordering.

Pasteurized Cow's Milk and Other Pasteurized Dairy Products

The majority of people are lactose intolerant; whether they know it or not. Children and adults on the autism spectrum disorder especially should avoid cow's milk because of the casein that is in cow's milk. Sensitivity to casein is also associated with depression and with skin problems, like acne and eczema. If you must use cow's milk, it should be raw and consumed in small amounts.

Soy

Soy food products are very unhealthy for mental and physical health UNLESS they are fermented. Unfermented soy contains "anti-nutrients," such as saponins, soyatoxin, phytates, trypsin inhibitors, goitrogens, and phytoestrogens. Phytic acid is found in high amounts in soy, and this suppresses digestive enzymes and thyroid function which can be associated with depression. Soy also suppresses pancreatic enzymes required for fat digestion. Another reason to avoid soy is that nonorganic soy is heavily sprayed with pesticides, and it is almost always genetically modified unless specifically labeled otherwise.

Acceptable forms of soy include: miso, shoyu, tamari, and tempeh, and then only in small quantities. Tofu, very occasionally, is acceptable.

Avoid: Soy milk, soy protein, soy burgers, and soy yogurts. Read food packages. Soy protein solates are often added to prepared meats, sausages and many packaged foods and should not be eaten.

Water for Well-Being

Water is essential for good mental health. Our bodies are really big balloons of water. Dehydration leads to fatigue and headaches, which can lead to taking pain killers or stimulants that in turn worsen mood. Dehydration also causes an excessive release of stress hormones, like cortisol, and contributes to food cravings.

Purifying Water

Water should be filtered if it contains impurities. Chlorine in drinking water causes vitamin E deficiency when consumed over a long term and kills beneficial bacteria in the gut.

There are different kinds of water purifiers. Activated charcoal filters remove toxins and wastes that are not water soluble, though they will not remove toxins like nitrates, nitrites, and sodium fluoride. Reverse-osmosis purifiers remove nearly all toxins, minerals, and gases and produce almost completely purified water.

Chemicals in plastic can seep out of plastic water bottles when left sitting out for a long time or if they are exposed to heat or sunlight. Even if they are BPA-free, the other chemicals in the plastic are dangerous and could disrupt endocrine function.

Water Tips for Mental Health

How do I know if I'm dehydrated?

Pinch the skin over the back of the hand. The skin should return immediately to its original position. Mild dehydration will show up as the skin returning a little more slowly.

How do I calculate my daily need for water?

Take 50% of your body weight. This number is how many ounces of water your body and mind needs each day. For example, if you weigh 150 pounds, you require 75 ounces of water.

How do I make sure I get enough water every day?

In the evening, fill up the required number of glass jars you need to drink for the next day, and place those jars around your home or office where you spend time. By the end of the day, all the jars should be empty. This way you know you'll have had your required water for the day.

Did you know that water retention (swelling at the ankles or feeling puffy and bloated) is often a sign of needing more water not less? The body holds onto water when it doesn't have enough.

Coffee: the Good, the Bad, and the Ugly

Coffee is a drug, not a beverage, so use it like one for its benefits, and eliminate it when necessary. Coffee is a great mood booster for depression and attention, but it makes anxiety worse. If you are anxious or have sleep challenges, then coffee should be the first drug to eliminate from your diet. Cold-Brewed and organic is the healthiest way to make coffee, because it cuts down on the acid, which can contribute to gastroesophageal reflux. Coffee should always be organic and cold-brewed.

Cold-Brewed Coffee

1. To reduce the acidity of your coffee by 70 percent, a cold-brewing method should be used to make both hot and iced coffee.
2. Start with coarsely ground, organic coffee. If you're grinding beans at the store, use the "French Press" setting.
3. Combine grounds with water in a glass container. Use ⅔ cup of grounds with 1½ cups of water at room temperature. Stir well.
4. Cover the container and let steep in a cool, dark place for 12-16 hours. Strain the mixture using a non-paper coffee filter or mesh strainer. You now have a concentrated coffee extract that should be mixed with hot water to taste.
5. To make iced coffee, mix equal parts coffee extract with cold water and add ice.
6. To make hot coffee, use equal parts coffee extract (at room temperature) and boiling water. These ratios can be adjusted depending on how strong you like your coffee.
7. Store your supply of cold brewed coffee in the fridge and make it fresh every week.

Kicking the Coffee Addiction

Assess how your coffee intake may contribute to anxiety and insomnia, and use the methods below to decrease or eliminate it from your diet.

Lowered Caffeine Method

Week 1: Instead of coffee, brew caffeinated coffee substitute, such as yerba mate, chai, black tea, or green tea (these will all have less caffeine than coffee and will help in the transition).

Week 2: Replace half of the caffeinated coffee substitute with a caffeine-free coffee substitute or herbal tea. There are many delicious herbal coffee drinks available, like Teeccino, Roastaroma, or Inka, that are made from ingredients like chicory root, dandelion root, and barley.

Week 3: Completely replace the caffeinated coffee substitute with a caffeine-free choice and hug yourself for overcoming the addiction!

Quick and Easy Method

Week 1: Replace ½ of your coffee with herbal tea or a caffeine-free coffee substitute.

Week 2: Brew just a ¼ of your original coffee intake and replace the rest with a caffeine-free choice.

Week 3: Drink only caffeine-free coffee substitutes or herbal tea and be free of caffeine!

Getting Started with Slow Cooking

A crock pot, or slow cooker, is a great way to begin cooking, and is also an easy cooking method when there is not enough time to prepare food. It is inexpensive and requires just an electrical outlet. Place protein (a whole chicken, or a beef or lamb roast) and vegetables, along with garlic, onions, and herbs, in the crock pot and set on low, cooking for 6-8 hours. Do this before bed and you have lunch and dinner ready the next day. Or prepare before leaving the house in the morning for dinner that night. Save the unused juices for your next soup or stew. Add sea salt near the end to season. Many of the protein recipes in these cards can be made in a slow cooker.

Time Guide: Converting conventional cooking times to crock pot times:

If Recipe Says:	Cook on Low:	Cook on High:
15 - 30 mins	4 - 6 hrs	1½ - 2 hrs
35 - 45 mins	6 -10 hrs	3 - 4 hrs
50 mins - 3 hrs	8 -18 hrs	4 - 6 hrs

Aromatherapy in the Kitchen and Office

Aromas alter moods, and there is no better place than the kitchen to infuse the home with aromas that quell anxiety and lift the mood. Here are a few simple tips for infusing your home with a relaxing, comforting aroma:

- Gently simmer a **cinnamon stick** in water to infuse the smell throughout your home or office.
- **Cloves** enhance mood and increase well-being. Pop a clove or two in your mouth to freshen breath after a delicious meal rich in garlic.
- Place 8 drops of **vanilla extract** in a half-cup of water. Simmer to infuse the air.
- Simmer **peppermint leaves** or oil to relieve tension and headaches, or to energize after a long day of work or study.
- **Orange, lemon, and lime** aromas all lift mood. Slice open a lime and inhale deeply, thinking about all the things that you are grateful for.
- Simmer **cardamom pods** in water to make your space feel relaxed.
- Place **fresh lavender** in a vase in a room where you wish to relax. Lavender may also be an ingredient in your recipes. Add it to your lemonade or include it in meat rubs along with other herbs and spices. Make sure to buy culinary lavender, not ornamental lavender, when using in recipes.

ANXIETY

The key to reducing anxiety is to eat foods that are calming and to eliminate foods that are stimulating. This can be managed with foods that provide grounding energy but relax the nervous system. Repeat your mantra: *"Food preparation is meditation, food preparation is relaxing."* These recipes will provide you with what you need to nourish the brain, mind, and body.

Green Tea Smoothie

Green tea is an ideal beverage to reduce anxiety while staying alert and focused. This smoothie is an excellent alternative to stimulant medications for people of all ages. It contains the anxiolytic amino acid theanine, which reduces the buzz provided by the caffeine. This smoothie can be eaten any time of day but preferably before 6 pm. I suggest using powdered Matcha green tea because it is richer in theanine, but you can also steep bags of green tea or loose leaf tea.

If you steep the bags, make a quart of concentrated tea ahead of time and keep it in the fridge to use when making this smoothie. The tea will last a week in the fridge. Experiment with the ingredients in this smoothie to suit your taste.

Ingredients

½ cup almond or hemp milk or whole milk yogurt (cow or goat)

¼ cup frozen blueberries or raspberries

1 tsp. matcha, green tea powder, or ½ cup concentrated green tea

3 drops liquid stevia or 1 tsp. raw honey to taste

Optional: half of a banana

Directions

• Blend in a blender until smooth.

TIP: Use stevia liquid; the powder can be bitter. Use honey sparingly but when you do, buy raw honey that is local to your neighborhood or region. It can also help reduce allergies and is anti-bacterial.

NOTE: If you use the green tea bags, steep 6 in a quart of hot water for 20 minutes. After you use the bags, save them in the fridge and apply them to your eyes while you rest to reduce inflammation or tired eyes.

Sleepy Time Oats

This recipe is the perfect late night snack for relaxation and sleep. The oats are anxiolytic and nuts provide some fat and protein to keep blood sugar stable through the night. Add just a few raisins for some sweetness.

Ingredients

2 cups steel cut oats
7 cups water

Directions

- Place the oats and water in a slow cooker, then cover and set on low for 6-8 hours. Eat some right away topped with raisins and chopped walnuts. The extra oatmeal will store
  in the fridge for a week. When you want quick steel cut oats, place a portion in a ceramic cup in a steamer pot and steam until hot, then serve.

- A half a cup (4 oz.) of good quality dark beer made with oats and hops is a mild nervine, anxiolytic, and muscle relaxant, and is also rich in B vitamins. Soak in a tub with warm water and add 1 cup of Epsom salts and lavender oil essence.

TIP: It is important to use whole oats, or steel-cut oats, not instant oatmeal. Make sure if you are gluten-sensitive/intolerant, that you obtain gluten-free oats (while oats do not contain gluten, they are often cross-contaminated with wheat). Steel-cut oats are rich in silicon, phosphorus, and magnesium, and provide a calming, nourishing effect. Sweeten them with a little blackstrap molasses to add iron, copper, magnesium, potassium, and manganese.

Thai Coconut Chicken Soup

This soup is warming and satisfying all at once. The benefits of chicken and chicken broth, coconut cream, and the herbs all contribute to elevate mood and increase a sense of satisfaction. Coconut is rich in B Vitamins, which reduce anxiety, and the fat is very easy to digest and supports memory and focus.

Ingredients

Half of a raw chicken

14 oz. coconut cream

1 stalk lemon grass (found at local Asian grocery, or use a ¼ tsp. powdered lemon grass)

5 slices fresh ginger

1 tsp. Thai red chili paste

Sea salt, to taste

For garnish: Equal parts chopped basil, cilantro, and green onions

Directions

- Place chicken in a pot and cover with water. Gently boil for 45 minutes (or until the meat falls off the bones). This liquid provides a rich broth.
- When finished cooking, set the chicken aside and add 14 oz. of the chicken broth to a soup pot. Add the coconut cream, lemon grass, and ginger.
- Take a quarter cup of the broth and place in a separate, small bowl. Dissolve the Thai red chili paste in the liquid, then add back to the soup pot.
- Simmer for 20 minutes and then use a slotted spoon to lift out the ginger and lemon grass. Add sea salt to taste.
- Bone the chicken and add the meat back into the soup. Serve in bowls and garnish with the fresh chopped basil, fresh cilantro, and chopped green onions.

NOTE: You may use coconut cream or coconut milk.

Greens with Creamy Miso Dressing

Greens with some fat make the perfect mental health meal. The greens help to detoxify the liver and emulsify and digest the various fats in this recipe so they can be used for brain energy. The white or yellow miso is the mildest. While it is often an acquired taste, it is one worth acquiring because it provides much needed healthy bacteria to enhance GABA, the relaxing neurotransmitter in the gut. Always choose full fat yogurt, for the benefits of the fat.

Ingredients

1 rounded tbs. white or yellow miso
2 tbs. rice wine vinegar
½ tsp. grated fresh ginger
1 small garlic clove, minced or put through a press
Pinch of cayenne
4 tbs. dark sesame oil
2 tbs. plain full-fat yogurt

Directions

- In a blender, mix all ingredients until smooth and creamy.

- Pour over greens and enjoy.

- Top a large bowl of fresh greens of your choice (arugula, romaine, red leaf, spinach, etc.) with a generous dollop of dressing and add raw sunflower seeds or pecans.

NOTE: This dressing will store for up to a week in the refrigerator.

Making Vinegar

Vinegar is an important fermented food that is easy to add to salad dressings or after your slow cooker meat and bone recipes are nearly done. It is also easy to make for a fun family activity. Vinegar increases energy and helps to reduce anxiety and depression.

To be medicinal, vinegar should be naturally made. It should have "a good enough mother." The mother is the cloudy bacteria that is fermented and is the most nutritious part of the vinegar. Apple Cider Vinegar is one of the best, but you can also have fun making fruit vinegars.

Make vinegar with almost any fruit: apples, pears, or raspberries. One of my favorites is pineapple. Plan ahead—when buying a pineapple for the fruit, save the rind to make the vinegar once you cut open the pineapple.

Ingredients

1 qt. glass jar, sterilized
3 cups filtered water
¼ cups coconut sugar or dark brown sugar
The rind of 1 organic pineapple
Piece of cheesecloth, to fit over mouth of jar

1 rubber band

Directions

- Scrub the rind of the pineapple and set the rind aside on paper towels to dry.

- Dissolve the sugar in a little water and then add pineapple scraps and rind to the sterilized jar until the jar has a few inches of room at the top.

- Place the cheesecloth over the mouth of jar with the rubber band.

- Place the jar in a dark cupboard, let it ferment for 4 weeks, opening container to lightly stir the contents daily.

- At 4 weeks, strain the contents through the cheesecloth into sterilized bottles and seal. Store in the refrigerator.

- Use it in your salad dressings along with olive oil, garlic and fresh herbs.

Vibrant Vinaigrette

Salad dressings are liquid medicine and the best ones are those that you make yourself. Making salad dressing is one of the first steps to take toward vibrant mental health and wellness. All commercial salad dressings use poor quality oils. You also want to avoid the additives, sugar, and synthetic ingredients in store-bought dressings. This dressing is especially good for anxiety. Apple cider vinegar increases energy, reduces depression and anxiety, and improves mood. This dressing is also good for the liver and gallbladder.

Make this dressing and keep it in a glass bottle in the fridge for up to 2 weeks.

Ingredients

1 cup cold-pressed extra-virgin olive oil
1 cup organic flax or hemp seed oil
3 cups organic apple cider vinegar
2 cloves freshly crushed garlic
1 tsp. of your favorite herb (dill, basil, oregano, caraway seed, etc.)

Directions

- Combine all of the ingredients except the herbs in a glass bottle, shake, and refrigerate.

- Use 4-6 tablespoons over salad or steamed broccoli or chard.

- Top with a different herb each time you pour the dressing, or top your salad with frozen raspberries.

Jamaica Chia Berry Balancer

This is a refreshing and uplifting substitute for soft drinks that are high in sugar and additives that lead to anxiety, plummeting mood, and low energy. The sugar and corn syrup in foods and drinks are inflammatory, and stopping their use is the first step to mental health.

Like berries, Roselle flowers, also called Jamaica (pronounced ha-my-ca) are rich in anthocyanins, the antioxidants that give berries their blue, purple, and red colors. They were brought to Jamaica from Africa and are used worldwide. They are known also for the popular *agua de Jamaica* in Mexico.

Mineral water called Lithia or mineral water like San Pellegrino, or Penafiel (from Mexico) contain trace amounts of the mineral lithium. Lithium is found naturally in mineral springs throughout the world and is an anti-anxiety mineral, a neuroprotective, helping to reset circadian rhythms (the wake-sleep cycle which is implicated in mood disorders, PTSD and Insomnia). Chia seeds are soothing to the mucus membranes and are a good source of energy and Omega 3 fatty acids.

NOTE: Find Jamaica (Roselle) in Mexican food stores or order online.

Make a concentrate of Jamaica so you can store it in the fridge or add hot water for tea. Boil 4 cups of water, turn off the heat and add 3 big handfuls of Jamaica calyces. Let sit for 15 minutes and strain. Add stevia to taste, but allow some tartness to shine through. Makes 2 servings

Ingredients

½ cup of Jamaica concentrate
½ cup frozen blueberries or raspberries
2 cups of sparkling mineral water
Ice
5 drops stevia extract

Directions

Mix the ingredients together and top with berries.

Variations: Instead of sparkling water and ice, use plain water and add 1 tsp of chia seed to the drink. Let sit 10 minutes until gelatinous and then drink. This is ideal for depression that also co-occurs with IBS, colitis, and GERD.

Delight-Full Dandelion Quiche

This recipe contains the right combination of good brain food: eggs, fats, greens, and wild rice. The practice of our ancestors of eating or drinking "bitters" after a meal was for just this purpose -- to help the food digest more efficiently.

Dandelions are a bitter green that we often ignore in our kitchen and often try to get rid of them in our yards. But rather than killing those medicinal greens, eat them. Dandelions pop up in the spring so we can spring clean our liver. Or make this as a nourishing winter dish. Look in your yard (or ask your neighbor), but make sure they are not sprayed. If you do not have dandelions, substitute chard, spinach or lambs quarters, or other greens that you find.

Ingredients

1½ cups water

¾ cup wild rice

5 eggs

3 tbs. Parmesan cheese, sheep or goat

4 tbs. goat feta cheese

4 tbs. Manchego or Parmesan cheese

4 cups wild dandelion greens

2 tbs. dried sweet basil

1 pinch pepper

1 pinch sea salt (to taste)

1 tbs. lemon juice

1 medium onion, sliced

1 tbs. olive oil

1 tbs. butter

½ cup organic full fat cream

Directions

- Place the water in a pan, add the rice and cover. Bring to a boil, then reduce heat as low as possible and let set for 20 minutes. Don't be tempted to lift the lid to check on the rice, as you will release the steam.
- When it's done, fluff the rice with a fork and mix with 1 beaten egg and 1 tablespoon grated cheese.
- Press firmly into a butter-greased pie pan, forming a crust. Press up along the walls so that it is about ¼ inch thick.
- Bake the crust for 15 minutes at 375° F.
- Remove from the oven and set aside.
- Steam dandelion greens in ¾ cup water in a covered pot for 4 minutes.
- Drain water off greens and chop to about 2-inch lengths.
- Add pepper and lemon juice. Set aside.
- Place sliced onions in a heated pan with olive oil and a teaspoon of butter.
- Cook for 5 minutes, then add the greens, pepper, and basil, and continue cooking until the mixture is well blended. Then squeeze on lemon juice.
- Combine remaining eggs, cheese, cooled greens mixture and cream in a bowl. Pour liquid carefully onto rice pie crust.
- Place pie on a cookie sheet and place in the preheated oven.
- Bake for 30 minutes at 375° F. When you can insert and remove a knife without batter sticking to it.
- Remove from the oven and let rest for 10 minutes. Serve.

NOTE: You can add a few teaspoons of organic smoked ham or bacon on top of the quiche before baking for additional flavor. For extra richness, grate about three tablespoons of Manchego or Parmesan on top of the pie after it is finished.

TIP: If you aren't used to eating bitter greens, it can take a while to develop a taste for them. You can always mix part dandelion and part spinach in this recipe to reduce the bitter taste, especially when feeding children.

Organic Slow Baked Beans

A meal to calm you down. These beans are tasty and especially nutritious with the addition of organic blackstrap molasses and anti-inflammatory spices. Blackstrap molasses is rich in B-6, magnesium, calcium, and potassium, all of which combine to produce a very calming meal. This recipe is easy to make with a slow cooker; start it in the morning, and by dinnertime a rich, healthy meal will be waiting.

Ingredients

2 cups dried organic pinto beans
1 onion, diced
1 clove garlic
2 tbs. olive oil
½ cup organic blackstrap molasses
1 6-oz. can tomato paste
2 tbs. yellow mustard

☒ 1 tbs. smoked paprika
☒ ¼ tsp. cayenne
☒ 1 tbs. grated turmeric root
☒ 1 tbs. Worcestershire sauce
☒ 1 tbs. organic apple cider vinegar
☒ 6 cups water
☒ Sea salt and pepper to taste

Directions

- Wash, rinse and soak the beans overnight. In the morning, rinse the beans and place in the slow cooker.

- Sauté the onion and garlic in the olive oil and add to the slow cooker along with the rest of the ingredients (save the salt and pepper until the beans are finished cooking).

- Cover with the water and cook on low for 4-6 hours.

- Salt to taste.

- Serve with coleslaw or a chopped green salad and Vibrant Vinaigrette.

Gluten-Free Apple Hazelnut Tart

This tart is simple to make and sweet and ideal for a gluten-free dessert. Hazelnuts are rich in healthy fats and support brain function. Apples, along with the pectin, is an ideal food for easy digestion.

Ingredients

1 cup hazelnuts (reserve 6 nuts)
2 eggs (duck or chicken)
¼ cup almond flour or rice flour
2 apples
½ tbs. pure fruit spread (raspberry, strawberry, or blueberry)
¼ cup water

Directions

- Grind hazelnuts into a fine flour and combine with the almond or rice flour in a bowl.
- Add two eggs and mix until moist.
- Place parchment paper inside a 9-inch pie plate and spread the crust mixture inside the pan.
- Bake for 3–5 minutes or until slightly cooked.
- Slice the apples into thin wedges and place in the baking dish, working from the edge to the center in a circular design.
- Add the water to the fruit spread to make a syrup.
- Pour and spread the syrup over the apples.
- Crush and sprinkle the remaining nuts over the tart and bake in the oven at 350° F for 20 minutes.

Culinary Herbs for Anxiety

Lavender

Lavender helps to relieve stress and anxiety, improves sleep and mood, and is used in treating depression. The dried buds can be used with other herbs on meat or fish (as in the herb blend, *Herbes de Provence*) or added to salads. Try adding the dried herb to dressings, teas, and baked goods.

Chamomile Tea /Te de Manzanilla

Called "little apple" because its fragrance is similar to that of an apple, chamomile tea is gentle and soothing for anxiety, muscle tension, and stress, and it also aids sleep. Traditionally used in Mexico to soothe belly aches in children and adults, it makes a soothing tea to drink when anxious or before bed. Chamomile can also be made as a cold beverage during the summer months, and the concentrated tea can be added to smoothies. Add a little raw honey or stevia to taste.

DEPRESSION

Food preparation is one of greatest self-care efforts we can make. Touching the food, breathing and smelling deeply, and connecting with others in the kitchen decreases the dissociation which gets in the way of our self-care. These recipes reduce inflammation which occurs with depression, support vital energy (especially the adrenal glands), and reduce fatigue.

Indonesian Avocado Chocolate "Moodshake"

This is a variation on a traditional Indonesian drink. This special combination of avocado, coconut and chocolate makes for a refreshing afternoon drink if your energy and mood start to drop. These three foods are easily absorbed and utilized by the brain, and the drink is delicious. Make this for your family, friends, and colleagues!

Ingredients

1 small ripe avocado

1 cup almond or coconut milk

¼ cup heavy organic cream or coconut cream

5 ice cubes

2-3 Tbs. organic cocoa (no sugar added)

5-10 drops of stevia (to taste)

Directions

- Add all the ingredients but the chocolate to a blender and process until smooth.

- Then add chocolate and stevia to taste.

- Optional: add half a frozen banana to the mixture.

Lemon Chicken Elation

This meal is a simple mood boosting meal that cooks itself. The aroma of lemon lifts a depressed mood, while the chicken stabilizes blood glucose, sustains energy and attention, and is also antibacterial and antiviral. Garlic is rich in sulfur which lifts mood, and the minerals from the slow cooked vegetables provide potassium, which enhances relaxation and supports adrenal function, thereby allowing you to adapt to stress.

Ingredients

1 whole organic/free range chicken (including neck and feet)

4 cups of water

4 stalks celery, sliced

3 medium carrots, sliced

4 small red potatoes diced or 2 sweet potatoes, diced

1 onion, diced

1 clove garlic, crushed

½ cup chopped parsley

Sea salt to taste

2 lemons

NOTE: You can make a variation on this soup by replacing the lemons with 1/2 cup of dry white wine. The alcohol cooks off and leaves a rich broth.

Directions

- Wash chicken and place whole (or quartered) in the slow cooker along with vegetables and liquids.
- Cook for 4 hours on high, or 8 hours on low.
- Add the parsley, salt and juice from 2 lemons, and grate 1 teaspoon of lemon zest on top before serving.

Cooking Tip: Never add salt or lemon until after the soup has finished cooking.

Pork Adobo

This classic recipe from the Philippines is one of the best dishes to eat to decrease anxious depression and increase energy. The combination of pork and vinegar provides an acid balance that will reduce fatigue and anxiety and lift your mood.

Ingredients

2 tbs. coconut oil

2 lbs. fresh pork shoulder or butt cut into bite size cubes or irregular shapes

8 cloves garlic, crushed

Water (enough to cover the meat)

1 cup white vinegar

1 tsp. sea salt

1 tsp. peppercorns

½ tsp. cloves

3 bay leaves

3 tbs. soy sauce

Directions

- Place oil in a large pot, add the pork and braise for 10 minutes.

- Add the garlic and stir. Then add just enough water to cover the pork.

- Add the vinegar, salt, peppercorns, cloves, and bay leaves. Place the lid and put on low heat for 2 hours, or until the pork is very tender.

- Serve hot in a bowl over Jasmine or brown rice.

Pesto and Brown Rice

Summertime is when basil can be found in large quantities at farmer's markets. This is the time to buy a few pounds of this mood altering herb and spend an afternoon with friends and family making pesto for everyone. You can freeze it in small containers and have basil throughout the winter months to your heart's delight.

Ingredients

½ cup pine nuts

⅓ cup virgin olive oil

1 cup water

1 tsp. spirulina

1 clove of garlic, minced

½ cup fresh basil

¼ cup fresh parsley

2 cups water

1 cup brown rice

Directions

- Place the pine nuts, olive oil, water, spirulina, and garlic in a food processor and pulse until smooth and creamy.

- Add the basil and parsley to the blender and pulse for 30 seconds.

- Place the water in a medium size pot and bring to a boil. Add the rice, turn the heat to low, cover, and cook for 45 minutes. Turn the heat off and let sit for an additional 10 minutes.

- Serve the pesto over the cooked rice.

NOTE: A less expensive alternative to pine nuts are walnuts, (the brain food *par excellence*) but they also have a slightly stronger flavor.

NOTE: When pinched for time, take a few tablespoons of the frozen pesto out of the freezer and stir into sautéed shrimp or into an omelet. Or take a piece of bread and cover it with pesto, grate some cheese on top and pop it under the broiler. Don't overcook the pesto. Let it dissolve and warm, but it does not need to cook.

Can't Beat These Beets

You either love beets or hate them. This recipe will help you start a love affair with them if you have yet to embrace this sweet smooth ruby red vegetable that is the best vegetable for the gallbladder. Why do I wax on about the liver and gallbladder so much? Because this dynamic duo helps us to digest the fats which then go to our brain and improve our focus and memory. Beets are rich in betaine which helps decrease PMS and depression.

Ingredients

Bunch of 4-6 beets (with fresh greens)
2 cups of organic Greek yogurt (or Labneh)
2 tbs. fresh mint
Pinch sea salt
Dash Aleppo pepper (or Cayenne)

Directions

- For this recipe, beets can be steamed or roasted. Wash the beets and cut off the fresh greens and set aside. Always cook beets with their jackets on.
- If steaming, place in a steamer pot with plenty of water (you will need to replenish) as medium to large beets can take an hour to cook. Never test if the beets are done by piercing them as it lets out the valuable juices. Time them for one hour and set them aside to cool. Once cooled, run them under cool water and the jackets will slide off. Set on a cutting board and slice 1-inch thick pieces. Place in the fridge to cool.
- Baking takes about the same amount of time as steaming. Wash the beets, then place some olive oil in your hands and cover the beets with the oil. Place in a baking dish and bake in the oven for 45-60 minutes (depending on the size of the beets) at 375° F.
- Now take the well-washed beet greens, chop them and add onion, olive oil, and garlic to a fry pan. Gently sauté until limp.
- Place several large dollops of Greek yogurt on a platter. Add the cold beets and season with salt. Top with fresh mint leaves.
- Take the hot beet greens and place them next to the yogurt. Top with salt and aleppo pepper. The hot and cold mixture is a delight to the senses and will convert anyone to the pleasure of beets.

Greek Salad Galore

This is one of my favorite salads; not only does it taste good but it's a meditation on chopping that relaxes the mind, and the crunch is so satisfying to the senses. Use this salad to enjoy the varieties of cold pressed olive oil that are available, especially the tangy organics from California. The dressing alone is medicine for the liver and gallbladder and can help to reduce anger and depression, while increasing energy and metabolism. Each time you prepare this salad you can vary the vegetables, but my favorite combination is below. Oregano and basil are anti-inflammatory and lift the mood while dill aids digestion.

Ingredients

2 large vine ripe tomatoes (diced)
4 small pickling cucumbers (diced)
¼ of a medium size red onion (diced)
1 red pepper (diced)
Bunch of fresh Italian parsley (chopped)
½ cup Kalamata or green olives (pitted)
Fresh dill (or dried)
Fresh oregano (or dried)

Fresh basil leaves
Greek sheep or goat feta cheese
Sea salt and pepper, to taste

Dressing

½ cup cold-pressed olive oil
2 lemons or limes, fresh squeezed
1 clove garlic, mashed

Directions

- Chop and dice all the ingredients, then gently mix them in a large bowl. Mix the dressing and add to the salad, tossing to cover all of the vegetables.
- Season to taste.

NOTE: To vary this dressing, you can replace the lemon with a splash of balsamic or ¾ cup of red wine vinegar.

Cooking tip: Throw away your garlic press and just place a garlic clove (skin on) on the cutting board and take the side of a wide bladed knife and crush the garlic with one fell swoop of a press. The skin comes off easily and you have garlic ready to use.

Live Long with Baked Sweet Potatoes

Sweet potatoes are rich in anti-depressant vitamins like Vitamins A, B6, and Niacin. Since they are naturally sweet, they are nourishing when overcoming an addiction to sugar, wheat/grain, alcohol, or drugs. They can be eaten hot or cold, mashed, fluffed, or sliced cold into salads. I bake a half dozen in advance and then can grab one for an on-the-go snack as needed. They are useful for addressing low blood sugar, and they make an ideal snack for children instead of sweets.

TIP: Don't forget to top with plenty of raw butter and salt; the Vitamin A and raw butter work together for better absorption.

Ingredients

Sweet potatoes (as many as desired)

Olive oil (as needed)

Directions

- Preheat the oven to 400° F.
  Rinse sweet potatoes and pierce them several times with a fork.

- Rub a light coating of olive oil over the skin and bake for 60 minutes or until soft.

Sweet Potato Mousse

Ingredients

2 previously baked sweet potatoes, skins peeled

½ cup fresh whole cream

5 drops stevia

1 tsp. organic cocoa powder

Directions

- Whip up the sweet potatoes and fresh cream in a food processor.

- Stir in the stevia.

- Place in wine glasses or small ceramic cups and top with cocoa powder.

- Chill and serve for dessert.

Tangy Turmeric Energy Balance

Depression often means low mood, low energy, and often physical pain and lethargy. This recipe is fun to make and will help reduce all of those symptoms, while providing a tasty approach to self-care.

Ingredients

1 orange, quartered and peeled
1 large carrot, scrubbed and coarsely chopped
1 cup coconut water or coconut milk
½ cup frozen mango chunks
1 tbs. shelled raw organic flax or hemp seeds
¾ tsp. finely grated peeled ginger
1½ tsp. finely grated peeled turmeric or 1 tsp. turmeric powder
Pinch of cayenne pepper (optional)
Pinch of sea salt

Directions

- Place the orange, carrot and coconut water in a blender and blend until smooth.

- Add the rest of the ingredients, blending as you add them.

Health Tip: If you don't mind a touch of bitter, add a teaspoon of the white pith of the orange. It is rich in flavonoids, which are good for circulation and heart health.

Gluten-Free Hazelnut Muffins

Some people are allergic to gluten and some are "sensitive" to gluten. In sensitive people, gluten can contribute to major depression, psychosis, chronic digestive distress and opiate-like reactions which result from peptides in the gluten. This is a simple muffin recipe that is very forgiving with substitutions and one that everyone will find tasty. The key to the texture is the flour blend. The muffins are rich in protein, derived from hazelnuts and eggs. They have a good balance of quality protein and sweetness, making them an ideal treat or snack for the road or children's lunch boxes. When shopping for agave, make sure you obtain the dark, nearly black agave or substitute another sugar like honey or molasses.

Ingredients

1¾ cups hazelnuts
1 tsp. baking powder
6 tbs. oat flour
¼ cup tapioca or potato flour
Dash of sea salt
2 eggs
2 tbs. rice vinegar

¼ cup agave syrup
⅓ cup grated hard goat or sheep cheese (Pecorino)*
½ to ¾ cup cool water, as needed
1 tbs. melted butter or coconut oil
1 cup fresh blackberries or raspberries

NOTE: If you do not eat cheese, simply leave this ingredient out.

Directions

- Place hazelnuts in a food processor and process into a fine flour. Measure the flour to make sure that you have 1¾ cups hazelnut flour. Anything extra can be set aside and saved for another use. Preheat oven to 350° F. Lightly grease a 2½ x 1¼-inch muffin pan with butter or coconut oil and set aside.

- Mix hazelnut flour, baking powder, oat flour, tapioca flour, and sea salt in a large mixing bowl and whisk together.

- Put one egg in a separate bowl, separate the yolk from the second egg and add it to the bowl. Save the egg white for another use or discard. Add vinegar and agave to the bowl and whisk together, add cheese and mix in.

- Combine egg mixture slowly into the hazelnut mixture. If the batter is too thick, add a little water while stirring. Mix in the melted butter or coconut oil. Add the berries.

- With a large spoon, fill each muffin cup about three-quarters of the way full (any size muffin tin can be used – smaller cups will make more muffins). Place any excess in cups to equally distribute.

- Place the muffin tin in preheated oven for 25-30 minutes. Insert a knife into the thickest muffin to test if the muffins are fully cooked.

- When the knife comes out without excess uncooked batter on the surface, the muffins are done.

- When fully cooked, remove muffins from the oven. Gently loosen the muffins from the pan if they are sticky. Place a tea towel over the top of the muffin pan, and gently turn the pan over so the muffins spill out onto the towel, leaving them on their tops to cool. Serve.

Chai Tea For Relaxed Energy

This stimulating tea has the added benefit of infusing the home with the warm relaxing aromas of ginger, cardamom, cloves, and cinnamon as it simmers.

Ingredients

3 cups water
1-inch piece of fresh ginger, coarsely chopped
1 tsp. cardamom pods
½ tsp. cloves
¼ tsp. black peppercorns
¼ tsp. nutmeg
1 cinnamon stick
2 bags black (Assam) tea
½ cup milk (coconut, almond, or rice, etc.) or cream
Sweetener of choice (honey, stevia, or agave), as desired

Directions

- Place the water and ginger in a medium size pot and bring to a boil. Reduce heat to medium and simmer for 5 minutes.
- Add the cardamom pods, cloves, black peppercorns, and cinnamon, and simmer for another 15 minutes.
- Strain the tea into a large bowl, reserving the spices and roots to use for another batch of chai. Add the black tea to the bowl and cover, steeping for 2-3 minutes.
- Remove the tea bags. Add the milk and gently heat over medium-low heat for 5 minutes, stirring to combine.
- Serve in individual cups and sweeten to taste using honey, stevia, or agave nectar.

Culinary Herbs for Depression

Saffron

Saffron is a traditional Persian remedy for depression; it reduces stress, improves mood, and protects against memory loss. Add it to rice, soups, and meat. Do not use it in high amounts or every day, and it should be avoided by those with bipolar disorder, as well as pregnant women.

Nutmeg

Nutmeg elevates mood, reduces anxiety, and aids sleep. It is especially helpful for sleep when used as aromatherapy. Use in baking, or simmer in water to catch the aromas. Because it has such a distinctive smell and flavor, use it as one of many approaches in your repertoire. It should be used in moderation (less than half a teaspoon per day) to avoid any toxic effects. When using it in cooking, buy the whole nut and grate it with a microplaner. While we often use nutmeg in cookies and cakes, try using it in vegetable dishes.

Spinach with Nutmeg

Ingredients

Two tbs. of butter
1 lb of spinach just washed, not dried
⅛ tsp. nutmeg

Directions

- Melt the butter in a covered pot and drop in the spinach (the combination of the butter and water droplets on the spinach will be enough to steam it).

- When the spinach is wilted, remove it from the pot and top it with the grated fresh nutmeg.

INSOMNIA

Insomnia is not just about not being able to fall asleep. It may be about waking up in the middle of the night when blood sugar drops. Eating carbohydrates and fats tend to relax and aid sleep onset, but when the problem is waking up, then one benefits from a little protein and a grain or fruit just before bed to sustain an even blood sugar. When combined with herbs that also relax, you have a plan for culinary sleep medicine.

Cherry Chamomile Slumber Smoothie

Drink this smoothie an hour before you want to go to sleep. Cherries and chamomile tea help induce sleep, and the mangos, seeds, and coconut will support blood sugar throughout the night so you can rest peacefully. Blueberries or frozen bananas make a good substitute for mangos.

Ingredients

1 cup almond or coconut milk
½ cup strong, cold chamomile tea
1 cup frozen (or fresh) cherries
1 cup frozen mangos
1 tsp. flax seeds (or flax seed oil or lemon flavored fish oil)
½ tsp. chia seeds
1 tbs. coconut cream or coconut oil
3 drops liquid stevia
1 drop vanilla extract (optional)

Directions

- Place all ingredients in the blender and blend until smooth.

- Keep a quart of strong chamomile tea in the fridge or make "chamomile tea ice cubes" to add to evening smoothies.

NOTE: Sip your smoothie while taking a magnesium sulfate (Epsom salt) bath or foot bath.

Red Sauce with Wine Over Rice Noodles

Often we feel like a rich, comforting Italian pasta meal, and then we think twice about the consequences! This recipe answers the problems of bloating and fatigue that can occur with a heavy pasta meal, but does not sacrifice any of the taste or satisfaction. It's also quick to make. Make plenty of the sauce and freeze what you don't use.

Ingredients

¼ cup olive oil

1 onion, diced

2 cloves garlic, crushed

½ lb. organic chopped sirloin (optional)

1 large can organic diced tomatoes

1 cup red wine

1 tsp. dried oregano, or fresh oregano to taste

¼ cup oil-packed sun-dried tomatoes, thinly sliced

¼ cup Kalamata olives, pitted and sliced

1 package of wide Thai rice noodles

Grated cheese to taste

Directions

- Place the olive oil, onion, and garlic in a medium saucepan on low heat. Gently stir for 5 minutes.

- Add the chopped organic sirloin.

- Add the tomatoes and all of the ingredients except the noodles. Cover and simmer on low for 30 minutes.

- During the last 10 minutes of cooking, bring a pot of water to a boil. When the water boils, add the rice noodles and immediately turn off the heat.

- Let the rice noodles sit in the water until al dente (about 10 minutes) and then strain the water. Plate and top with sauce and grated cheese.

NOTE: Rice noodles do not require as much cooking time as wheat pasta.

Almond Tofu Saute

Tofu should be eaten only on special occasions. This dish can be made for that rare moment when you need a nutritious and delicious meal ready in a hurry. The fun thing about tofu is that once frozen and thawed it becomes like a sponge that soaks up all the flavors. You may also use it fresh so it is smooth and plumps up as it steams in the pan. I like to vary it according to my mood. Keeping a carton in the freezer, along with the ingredients below, ensures a quick meal at a moment's notice.

Ingredients

3 tbs. coconut oil
16 oz. firm tofu cubed into 1 inch pieces
2 tbs. gluten-free Tamari
1 bunch organic spinach, chopped
1 cup fresh pea pods
1 tbs. toasted sesame seeds
2 tbs. chopped green onions

Almond Butter Sauce

½ cup of almond butter
2 tbs. apple cider vinegar
½ cup warm water
Pinch of cumin seeds, ground cloves, and cardamom

Directions

- Heat up the coconut oil in a large frying pan to a medium heat and add the tofu. Stir gently with a rubber or silicon spatula, being careful not to break the tofu cubes.

- Add the tamari and stir so the tofu is coated. Cover and cook for 10 minutes until the tofu plumps.

- Layer the chopped spinach over the tofu and the pea pods over the spinach. Turn off the heat and cover for 5 minutes, letting the steam cook the vegetables.

- While the vegetables finish cooking, make the sauce. Add the almond butter, apple cider vinegar, water, and cumin seeds together to make a paste and set aside.

- Gently fold the almond butter sauce into the tofu and vegetables.

Serve over baked or steamed butternut squash or spaghetti squash. Top with toasted sesame seed and chopped green onion.

Optional: A variation on this dish is to add a can of heated coconut cream just before adding the vegetables and cook for 5 minutes. Add it at the last minute and top with chopped green onions.

Cooking Tips: Let the frozen tofu thaw and then hold it over the sink and gently press the water out working the corners and middle until the excess water leaves you with a wrung out sponge-like square. Then it is ready to cut into 1-inch cubes.

The trick to a quick non-grain side dish like squash is to bake the squash ahead of time, cube it and keep it in the fridge. You can heat it up by steaming it, adding what you need.

Broccoli Slaw with Cherries

Cherries are the best go-to food for aiding sleep. Keep dried organic cherries in the cupboard, frozen cherries in the freezer, and some cherry juice on hand. This versatile crunchy salad will tire you out just from the chewing!

Ingredients

1 large head of broccoli
2 carrots
1 apple (Granny Smith)
½ cup raw, or lightly toasted, almonds
Fresh mint leaves
1 cup dried cherries (no sugar)

Yogurt Dressing

¾ cup full fat goat or Greek plain yogurt
¼ cup organic mayonnaise
1 tbs. lemon juice
Sea salt (to taste)
¼ tsp. cayenne pepper, optional
¼ cup finely chopped shallot or red onion
1 tbs. fresh fruit or apple cider vinegar

Directions

- Wash and trim the broccoli and cut florets away from the stems. Thinly slice the florets and cut into small, bite-size pieces. Peel the stems and coarsely grate them, along with the carrots and apple. Toss together in a large bowl, then add the almonds, mint, and cherries.

- Mix the yogurt, mayonnaise, lemon juice, salt and cayenne pepper in a bowl. Add chopped shallot or red onion and apple cider vinegar. Whisk together until smooth. Pour the dressing over the slaw and toss.

- Cover, chill and serve.

Fish Cakes with Caper Sauce

This dish is sleep medicine. Canned fish, like pink salmon from Alaska, is a very cost efficient way to get the benefits from salmon (including omega 3s). Omega 3 fatty acids are relaxing and aid sleep. Capers are edible flower buds that are often found pickled in jars. They are rich in antioxidants and will help move you toward slumber. This sauce can be made with capers or with sour pickles.

Ingredients

1-1.5 lbs. canned salmon or cod
⅓ medium onion, finely chopped or grated
2 stalks celery, finely chopped
1-2 tbs. parsley, chopped (including stems)
1 tbs. organic mayonnaise (commercial or homemade)
½ tsp. yellow mustard

1 tbs. olive oil or avocado oil
2 tbs. buckwheat flour (or rice flour)
2 eggs (small to medium whipped with 1 tsp. of water)
Pepper to taste

Directions

- Place all ingredients in a medium to large bowl and blend until there is a batter (not thick, but enough to hold together in a large serving spoon).

- Heat a nonstick skillet (not Teflon, but a heavy bottom pan) to medium high and, using a tuna fish can "mold" (opened at both ends), drop about a ½ to ¾ inch layer of batter into the pan. As it begins to set, lift the mold and place on a cutting mat, then repeat.

- Continue until all batter has been used in this round. Turn each patty when set, and once firm to the touch, remove each to a warm pan and complete the process with the remaining batter. (Should make 8-12 fish cakes).

- Serve warm.

NOTE: You may use fresh or canned crab, salmon, cod (or salt cod desalted), clams (butter clams, razor, minced), or any other firm and flavorful sea food.

Caper Sauce Ingredients

2 tbs. Greek yogurt

1 tbs. mayonnaise

1 tsp. dill (dried)

1½ tsp. capers or sour pickles chopped

1 tsp. onion finely chopped

Directions

- Combine ingredients and blend well.

- Place in the refrigerator for 30 minutes to cool and blend. Serve on top of fish cakes.

Polarity Tea

Insomnia, stress, and depression often go together because of the disruption in the Hypothalamic-Pituitary-Adrenal Axis. Basically this means that our sleep-wake cycle gets out of rhythm with the day-night cycle. Licorice tea will help to rest your day-night rhythm. Drink this in the morning to have a positive effect by night.

Ingredients

1 oz. licorice root (pieces)
1 oz. fennel seed
1 oz. fenugreek seed
2 oz. flax seed

Directions

- Mix the ingredients together while dry.
- Take 1 tsp. of the mixture and simmer it in approximately 2 cups water.
- Strain and drink. The recommended dosage is 2 cups per day.

Verdelicious Soup

This soup is a delicious way to eat a high chlorophyll meal and stimulate the palate. Verde means green in spanish and kids love this soup. They may not eat these same greens if served steamed on a plate. The fat in the soup aids the absorption of the minerals from the greens and provides a soothing, light meal to aid sleep. The broth can be prepared ahead and frozen, using the trimmings collected from raw vegetables.

Ingredients

1 bunch chard or spinach, coarsely chopped

1 bunch kale, coarsely chopped

4 to 5 onion greens, cut into inch pieces

½ cup loosely packed cilantro, coarsely chopped

1 medium sweet potato, chopped

1 medium yellow onion, chopped

3 tbs. olive oil

3 tbs. dry sherry (optional)

1 to 2 cloves garlic, finely chopped

2½ to 3 cups fresh vegetable broth

Freshly ground black pepper, to taste

1 tsp. pink or grey sea salt, to taste

Pinch smoked paprika

1 tbs. fresh lemon juice, or more to taste

Avocado, sliced in ½ inch wedges

Directions

- Wash the greens, trim off their stems, and slice the leaves. Combine the chard or spinach, kale, green onions, and cilantro in a large soup pot with 3 cups water and a teaspoon of salt.

- Add the sweet potato. Bring the water to a boil, turn to low, cover, and let simmer for about 30 minutes.

- While the soup simmers, heat the olive oil in a skillet. Sauté the yellow onion and garlic with a sprinkle of salt over medium heat, stirring occasionally, until it is slightly caramelized (about 10 minutes).

- Pour a splash of sherry onto the onions to deglaze the pan at the end.

- Add the caramelized onion and garlic to the soup.

- Add enough of the vegetable broth to make the soup pour easily.

- Puree the soup in the blender, in batches, being careful not to over-process.

- Return the soup to the pot, bring it back to a simmer, and taste.

- Add a pinch of salt and freshly ground pepper to taste, then add a pinch of cayenne and a tablespoon of lemon juice.

- Stir well and taste again.

- Garnish with a thin drizzle of olive oil.

- Top with sliced avocado.

Watermelon Gazpacho

This cold soup is refreshing and naturally sweet. Watermelon boosts mood and aids sleep. This soup is rich in easily assimilated minerals and makes an attractive raw meal for children and adults. Use only large, organic watermelons with seeds, not the small hybrid, seedless variety. The seeds will grind up and they add a vitamin-rich crunch to the soup.

Ingredients

6 cups watermelon, peeled, cut 2 cups into 1-inch cubes and put aside
2 cups ripe tomatoes, cubed
1 red bell pepper, diced
3 small pickling cucumbers, peeled and chopped
½ cup chopped red onions
1 jalapeño pepper, finely chopped (optional)
3 tbs. sherry wine or balsamic vinegar
3 tbs. extra-virgin olive oil

6 tsp. chopped fresh herbs: choose from dill, basil, mint, or parsley
1½ tsp. sea salt
½ tsp. freshly ground black pepper

Garnish

1 ripe avocado, peeled and diced
1 tsp. lemon juice
1 tsp. extra-virgin olive oil
Sea salt to taste

Directions

- In a blender or food processor, puree half of the watermelon, leaving the other half in chunks to add to the soup. Transfer to a large mixing bowl.

- Add the rest of the chopped vegetables to the bowl.

- Stir in vinegar, oil, herbs, salt, and pepper. Stir and place in the fridge for up to 24 hours before eating.

- To make the garnish, combine sliced avocado with lemon juice, olive oil, a sprinkle of salt and a pinch of pepper.

- To serve, fill individual soup bowls and garnish each with a dollop of chopped avocado.

Baked Pears with Walnuts

Ancient wisdom suggests that foods that look like a body part are medicine for that part. No food looks more like the brain than the walnut. Walnuts help with insomnia, which often occurs as part of depression. Combined with pears, whose skins are rich in powerful anti-inflammatories, this dish is a light, yet elegant dessert or snack that is ideal to eat before bed. Often if we wake in the night it is because we need some brain fuel. The combination of fructose, protein and fat in this recipe will enhance your slumber.

Ingredients

1 tbs. butter

4 pears

Raw walnuts (handful)

Raisins (handful)

1 tbs. maple syrup

Directions

- Grease a glass baking dish with butter. Preheat the oven to 350° F. Wash and dry the four pears. Slice them down the middle and scoop out the seeds, making a small center hole in the pears to hold raisins and walnuts. Place the pears (cut-side up) in the baking dish.

- Take a mixture of raw walnuts and raisins, and place it in the hollowed out area of each pear.

- Drizzle a few drops of maple syrup over each of the pears.

- Bake uncovered for 30- 45 minutes.

- Let cool. Eat as is or add a scoop of yogurt or drizzle coconut milk over the warm pears.

Culinary Herbs for Insomnia

Lemon Balm

Lemon balm has a delicate flavor that makes a good addition to food, tea, or aromatherapy. Research has shown that lemon balm has a relaxation effect and aids sleep, likely due to its effect on the Neurotransmitter GABA. It has been found to reduce anxiety and aid sleep in people with Alzheimer's.

Lemon Balm Tea Concentrate

Steep 1 cup of fresh lemon balm in 2 cups of boiled water for 20 minutes. Strain and add raw honey and store in the fridge. Take 1-2 tablespoons of lemon balm concentrate before bed.

Lemon Balm Butter

Chop a handful of leaves and add them to a $\frac{1}{8}$ lb of butter. Add some honey and store in a small tub in the fridge. If you cannot sleep, put some of the butter on a cracker or piece of bread. The combination of the lemon balm, fat and carbohydrate will help you fall asleep.

Salsa ————————•

Ingredients

Bunch of cilantro, finely chopped
4 Roma (plum) tomatoes, chopped into
small cubes
¼ of a red onion, chopped
¼ serrano chili, finely chopped (optional)
Top an avocado, or baked potato, or store
in the fridge and fold into your next omelet.

Cilantro (coriander)

People either love or hate cilantro. Also known
as Chinese parsley, its powerful flavor suggests
a potent medicine. It settles upset stomachs,
is antibacterial, and aids sleep. It makes a
good topping on avocados, salads, and soups.
Cilantro makes a good pesto and is essential
in salsa. Don't forget the stems, where most
of the flavor is concentrated.

ATTENTION & FOCUS

We need nourishment to pay attention and to focus for sustained periods. These recipes are designed especially to support you during the morning and through the afternoon, or anytime brain power is required. Many of these recipes are ideal for children whose attentional issues may be the lack of the right fuel combination for their uniquely creative brain.

Cashew-Apple Smoothie

Cashews and apples are a perfect combo for focus and attention. Bananas are rich in tryptophan which also lifts mood and supports focus. Make this recipe a "family affair" by asking family members to help make these smoothies and contribute their ideas for variations.

Ingredients

2 tbs. raw organic cashews
One quarter of a sweet apple,
coarsely chopped
Half of a banana
3 tbs. organic full-fat coconut milk
¼ cup coconut yogurt, dairy yogurt,
or kefir
½ cup milk of choice (hazelnut,
almond, hemp, etc.)
1 tbs. ground flax seeds
1 tbs. chia seeds

Directions

- Add all ingredients to a blender, in the order they are listed, and blend until smooth.

Repose Mineral Broth

Repose mineral broth increases energy, restores adrenal health, and reduces fatigue, high blood pressure, and water retention. Most modern diets provide a high sodium-to-potassium ratio, whereas traditional diets, like those of our ancestors, had at least twice the potassium to sodium. This imbalance contributes to fatigue, stress, anxiety, and high blood pressure.

Under stress, we require a lot more potassium to support our adrenal glands, which in turn support energy and good mood.

This broth can be made with the vegetable ends and pieces you don't use when cooking throughout the week. Save carrot tops, ends of onions, and other veggies in a container for a few days until you have enough to make this soup.

The cayenne pepper (it's really a fruit!) will provide a little pep to your mood and is helpful for digestion. Add a little white miso at the end to provide some healthy bacteria for your gut, and thereby enhance GABA, the relaxation neurotransmitter.

Ingredients

2 qts. water

2 large potatoes, chopped or sliced to approximately ½-inch slices

1-2 cups carrots, shredded or sliced, greens and all

1-2 cups celery, chopped or shredded, leaves and all

Handful of beet tops, turnip tops, parsley, onion, or whatever you have from the garden or left over from salads or cooking during the week.

2 cloves crushed garlic

Fresh herbs like sage, rosemary, thyme, and a Pinch of cayenne pepper (optional)

¼ tsp. mineral-rich sea salt (supports adrenal function)

1 tsp. miso (optional)

Directions

- Place all ingredients (except fresh herbs, cayenne, sea salt, and miso) in a large stainless steel, enamel, glass, or earthenware pot. Cover and cook slowly for about 1 hour.

- After the vegetables are finished cooking, add fresh herbs like sage, rosemary, thyme, and a pinch of cayenne pepper and sea salt.

- Strain the broth off, then add a teaspoon of miso after the broth is finished cooking. Serve warm or as a cool drink. If not used immediately, keep in the refrigerator and warm up before serving.

You can also use this as a base for any soup to enhance its nutritional value. Freeze it in containers and add to the slow cooker when making soups.

Cooking Tip: Miso is a very versatile food made from fermented beans or grains. Start with a mild-tasting miso, like white or barley miso. Never boil miso as it will kill the healthy bacteria. Always add it to soup after you have turned off the heat.

Shopping Tip: Not enough vegetables for your broth? The local food coop often has a "seconds basket" of two day old veggies that are inexpensive and perfect for this broth.

Health Tip: Use this broth as a base for making a beefy bone broth to uplift mood or energy, and for all addiction recovery.

Organic Hard-Boiled Eggs

I make a dozen hard boiled eggs each week and store them in the fridge so that I can grab 1-2 each day when I go on the road or need a quick snack. They are also easy to send with children as snacks during the school day. It is best to use eggs that are a few days old as this will make them easier to peel.

Ingredients

Organic farm eggs

Pinch sea salt

Dash vinegar

Directions

- Place the eggs in a saucepan and cover with an inch or two of cold water.

- Add a little salt, which can prevent the eggs from cracking, and a dash of vinegar which will help to keep whites from running out of eggs that might crack.

- Turn the heat on high and bring the water to a boil. Reduce the heat and boil for 1 minute. Remove from the heat and cover; let the eggs sit for at least 12 minutes.

- Remove the eggs with a slotted spoon and place in ice water. Let them sit until they are cool. Place in covered container in the fridge and use within 5 days.

Cooking Tip: To peel hard-boiled eggs, drain the cooking water after boiling and shake the pot from side-to-side until the shells crack. Fill the pot with ice water to cover the eggs and wait for them to cool.

Salmon with Sriracha Sauce

Salmon is the quintessential brain food. Whether fresh, cooked, raw, or canned, this fish should be a staple of your weekly diet. It is worth making a trip to the Pacific Northwest or Alaska to fish and eat salmon to your heart's (and brain's) content. Many people think it is difficult to cook salmon correctly. The key is not to overcook it. Salmon can be eaten a little pink (raw) on the inside as well.

Ingredients

1 large filet of wild salmon

3 tbs. mayonnaise

1 tsp. honey

2 tbs. Sriracha sauce

1 tbs. wheat-free soy sauce

½ tsp. garlic powder

Pinch of sea salt and pepper

Directions

- Place the large, thick filet of wild salmon on a cookie sheet.

- Preheat the oven to low broil.

- Make the sauce just before broiling the filet. The sauce is very forgiving so feel free to play with the quantity of ingredients to suit your taste.

- Mix the mayonnaise, honey, sriracha, garlic powder, salt and pepper until blended. Apply a layer to cover the filet.

- Place the cookie sheet with salmon on the middle rack (not too close to the broiler).

- Bake for about 15 minutes and then turn on the broil setting for the last 5 minutes. Keep a close eye on it while it broils.

- If you make extra salmon, you can put it in the fridge and top your salad with it the next day.

Cooking Tip: To test whether salmon is cooked, press with your forefinger on the thickest part of the salmon. If it stays down, cook it longer. If it rises back up, it is cooked. Fish continues to cook once out of the oven so do not over-cook.

TIP: If you like a little more spice than sriracha, add a pinch of cayenne pepper to the sauce. Cayenne stimulates digestion and enhances circulation.

Stewed Chayote

Chayote, also called a vegetable pear, is an ancient vegetable that is among the traditional foods originating in Mexico. A member of the squash family, it is versatile and very mild in flavor, which makes it an ideal balance to the strong flavors in this recipe. Rich in B-Vitamins and antioxidants essential for brain health, chayote is a humble vegetable that will not disappoint. It is available in Mexican food markets and most large chain grocery stores.

Chayote is best peeled under cold running water as it has a sticky sap that can irritate the skin. Peel as you would a cucumber and then slice in half, removing the inner seed. Then slice and cut into 1-inch cubes and set aside in a bowl.

Ingredients

2 tbs. olive oil

1 clove garlic

½ white onion

Small serrano chili

½ cup raisins

2 chayote, diced into 1-inch cubes

¾ cup white wine

¼ cup pine nuts (can substitute raw green pumpkin seeds)

Salt and pepper to taste

Directions

- Heat up the oil gently and add the garlic, onion,
  and half a serrano chili (de-seeded).
- Let cook for a few minutes and then add the raisins, chayote and white wine.
- Cover and simmer on a low heat for 15 minutes. The chayote will be firm and crunchy, but tender when ready.
- While the chayote is simmering, toast the pine nuts (or pumpkin seeds) until brown.
- For the last few minutes, uncover the chayote so the wine cooks off. Add salt and pepper.
- Pour the chayote into a serving bowl and top with the nuts.

Cooking Tip: My friend Alicia taught me this old Mexican trick to avoid the after effects of chili oil on your hands that can sting the eyes. After finishing working with the chili, do not wash your hands. It will only spread the oil. Instead, rub your hands through your hair (if bald, find someone else's hair!). The hair will absorb the oil perfectly.

Savory Baked Tart

Ingredients

2 tbs. olive oil

1 white onion, sliced into thin half-moons

1 lb. mix of chard and spinach

3 eggs, beaten

½ cup prepared masa*, loosened with

⅓ cup water

1 tsp. cumin seed, toasted and ground

Chopped herbs (cilantro, parsley, marjoram)

Sea salt, and pepper to taste

Directions

- Preheat oven to 350° F.
- In a cast iron skillet, slowly cook onions in a tablespoon of the oil until browned and fragrant.
- In a separate skillet, slowly sweat the chard and spinach in the remaining oil until wilted and tender.
- Remove and let cool; then wring all possible moisture from the greens.
- In a large bowl, mix together the eggs, prepared masa, cumin, herbs, and salt until blended.
- Fold in the greens. Add mixture to the skillet with the onions; stir to incorporate.
- Bake in preheated oven 30–35 minutes until browned and set. Let cool and then remove from pan to serve. Accompany with a tomato, cucumber and olive salad and vinaigrette.

* Masa Harina is Mexican corn flour.

Lemon Avocado Smoothie

The combination of fruits and vegetables in this smoothie make it both filling and tasty. This smoothie appeals even to children who avoid vegetables, and is a great way to introduce them to the joys of greens.

Ingredients

½ organic pineapple

2 to 3 organic lemons

1 banana

2 avocados

Handful of organic greens, such as spinach

Directions

- Slice the rinds off the lemons and pineapple (save for fruit vinegar). Cut into small pieces and run through a juicer to separate the juice from the pulp.

- Combine pineapple/lemon juice, banana, avocados, greens, and coconut oil in blender, and blend until smooth.

The Best Most Satisfying Chicken Wings

These wings make a whole meal and give the brain what it needs to accomplish a task.

Ingredients

2 lbs. chicken wings

2-3 cups of water

¼ cup toasted organic sesame oil

¼ cup Tamari or wheat-free soy sauce

¼ cup honey (optional)

1 piece of ginger, chopped (about 1 tbs.)

1 clove of garlic, crushed

Finely chopped lettuce or cabbage
for serving

1 cup cubed pineapple

1 cup of broccoli florets

Directions

- Wash and dry the chicken wings.

- Cut and separate the drumette from the wingette and cut off the tip.

- Place the chicken in a steamer pot with 2-3 cups of water.

- Bring to a boil, then reduce the heat and cover. Steam for about 20-30 minutes so the wings are nearly completely steam-cooked.

- While the wings are steaming, place the oil, soy sauce, honey (if using), ginger, and garlic in a large mixing bowl.

- When the wings are done, transfer them to the bowl with the oil mixture and rub on the wings so they are fully covered.

- Place a large fry pan on low heat and place the wings to cook covered for 15 minutes.

- Take the cover off for the last 5-10 minutes to concentrate the sauce. At this time, add the pineapple and broccoli so they are cooked but do not become too soft.

- Transfer the hot chicken wings to a platter of finely chopped lettuce or cabbage where the hot wings and sauce will wilt the greens. Garnish and serve.

NOTE: You have lots of options for a garnish: chopped green onions, toasted sesame seeds, sriracha sauce, or sprinkle fresh lime onto the chicken wings. Leftover wings can be placed in the fridge and are a great snack the next day.

Leslie's "Go-To" Granola

This recipe can be served for breakfast, and it also makes a snack for children at school or for adults at work. Have fun varying the types of nuts or dried fruit you use to keep this recipe new and interesting. Most store bought granola (and granola bars) has sugar, dried fruit with preservatives, and grains, which can contribute to lack of attention.

Making this granola is a great way to engage children in cooking adventures by having them choose their favorite nuts and dried fruits, and help to toast the granola. Note that there is a very small amount of gluten-free oatmeal added to this granola, but you can leave it out if you prefer. The sweet taste comes from the dried fruit, so there is no need to add extra sweetner.

Ingredients

To be cooked on the stovetop

½ cup raw pecans, lightly chopped

½ cup raw almonds, chopped or sliced

½ cup raw walnuts, chopped

½ cup gluten free oatmeal

½ cup extra virgin coconut oil, melted

Keep Raw

½ cup organic raisins

½ cup chia seeds

½ cup of chopped dates

½ cup shredded coconut (optional)

½ cup of organic, grain sweetened chocolate chips (optional)

½ cup of dried candied ginger (dust off extra sugar) (optional)

Directions

- Combine the stove top cooked ingredients in a large mixing bowl.

- Melt the coconut oil over a low heat and pour over this mixture.

- Place a large frying pan on the stove over a very low heat. Place a layer of this mixture in the pan and stir constantly until it becomes a light brown. You are toasting this mixture, but do not overcook.

- Remove from heat and place in a large bowl and toast the next batch.

- Do this until all the mixture is toasted. Then add the rest of the raw ingredients to the mixture and let sit until cool.

- Store in glass jars with tight lids in a dark cabinet.

NOTE: Make sure you purchase no preservative, no sugar-added dried fruits.

Cooking Tip: An option to toasting on the stovetop is to bake a thin layer on a cookie sheet at 350° F. However, it can tend to toast unevenly and too much. Experiment to see what works best for you.

Berry Crisp

Overuse of sugar and refined carbohydrates contributes to, and exacerbates, attention and focus challenges. This is a quick and healthy dessert to satisfy a sweet tooth and avoid those negative effects. It is sweet, satisfying, and medicinal. Use a mix of huckleberries, blueberries, blackberries or strawberries gathered during the summer, or use frozen berries during the winter.

Ingredients

⅓ tsp. stevia (sweet leaf) extract

1 tbs. arrowroot (optional)

¼ tsp. sea salt

¼ tsp. cinnamon

¼ tsp. nutmeg

1 tbs. lemon juice

4 cups berries

1 cup berry juice (drained from the fruit)

½ cup hazelnut flour

12 tbs. organic butter

¼ cup hazelnuts (cracked)

Directions

- Combine stevia, arrowroot (optional), salt, and spices in a saucepan.

- Add lemon and berry juices.

- Stir until smooth.

- Cook over low heat until thickened and clear, stirring constantly.

- Stir in berries and pour the mixture into a round glass baking dish or an enamel cast iron pan.

- Combine the hazelnut flour with the chunks of butter, maple sugar, and cracked hazelnuts, to form a dry chunky mixture. Sprinkle over the berries to form a topping.

- Place the dish in a 375° F oven for 30 minutes or until topping is slightly browned, and serve with hot tea.

Culinary Herbs for Attention and Focus

Both these herbs can be combined when making sauces, roasted potatoes, or roast pork.

Rosemary

Rosemary is an effective herb for improving concentration and memory, both as an essential oil and as a culinary herb. It can be used in cooking, made into a tea, or taken as capsules. Rosemary oil is also excellent for aromatherapy.

Sage

Sage is high in Vitamin K and also helps to improve memory and concentration. Sage can also be made into a tea or dried and burned for its purifying aroma and smoke.

ADDICTIONS

We all self-medicate. We all seek altered states of consciousness. The important question to ask: *"Is this 'medicine' good for me or harmful?"* The recipes in this section address the two intersecting phases of addiction recovery: detoxifying from the addiction and then providing the whole being with nourishing brain support.

Smooth Mood

Smoothies are a perfect food to use when withdrawing from drugs, alcohol, or pharmaceuticals. They provide an easy way to ingest nutrients and oils from vitamins and minerals, as an alternative to taking pills and capsules. Capsules can be opened and pills can be ground in a mortar and pestle, or in a small electric grinder. Experiment with ratios and quantities as well as fruits and base liquids. For a simple meal, or when digestion is impaired, add whey or rice protein powder as an easily digested source of protein; however, ensure it is made without sugar or additives.

Add the following to a blender:

4 oz. plain yogurt (goat) or almond, hemp, or raw milk (without sugar or fruit additives, water, or unsweetened fruit juice)

2 tsp (heaping) of liquid fish oil (2000 mg of omega-3 fatty acids)

¼ frozen banana (peel bananas and place in freezer ahead of time)

¼ cup frozen raspberries, blueberries, mangos, or fruit of choice

3-10 drops liquid stevia (optional, to taste)

½ tsp green tea powder

Powdered nutrients (like amino acids, vitamins and minerals)

Powdered whey protein (optional)

Water

Ice Cubes

Directions

- Add enough water and ice cubes so that it's either a drink or a thick frozen shake, experimenting with the amount of water.

Coconut-Sweet Potato Mood Stabilizer Soup ————————

Combining coconut and sweet potatoes provides a satisfying meal. The coconut is a nearly complete food, rich in healthy fat and protein for the brain and mind. The sweet potatoes are high in Vitamin A and support the immune system under stress. They also satisfy a sweet tooth, making this meal ideal for satiety, hypoglycemia, and recovery from sugar addiction. Children love the food combinations in this meal and will have fun toasting the coconut for the garnish.

Add the following to a blender:

8 cups of chicken broth (or substitute 4-8 cups of fresh vegetable broth if vegetarian)

2 cans organic coconut milk or coconut cream

3 (1-inch) pieces fresh ginger

1 onion, chopped

1 tsp. lime zest

1 stalk lemongrass, cut in chunks

¼ tsp. sea salt

4 Red Garnet sweet potatoes, cut into chunks

Juice from one lime

Fresh cilantro, chopped for garnish

Toasted shredded (no sugar) coconut, for garnish

Directions

- Prepare the broth ahead of time.

- In a 6-quart pot, bring the broth, coconut milk, ginger, onions, lemongrass, and ¼ teaspoon sea salt to a gentle boil and cook for about 20 minutes over medium heat. Reduce the heat to low and cook another 30 to 40 minutes.

- Remove the lemongrass. Add the sweet potatoes and turn the heat back up to medium, cooking for another 15 minutes.

- In a blender, purée small batches of the broth and sweet potatoes until smooth. Do not overfill the blender.

- Repeat until all of the soup is blended.

- Gently reheat the soup on the stove.

- To serve, ladle into soup bowls, squeeze some fresh lime juice over the top, and garnish with the cilantro and toasted shredded coconut.

NOTE: An alternative to the sweet potatoes is to use 2 large plantains.

Beet Arugula Spinach Salad

Beets are one of the best foods to help overcome addiction. They are sweet and soothing and they are very versatile; top hot beets with butter or blend them cold in a soup. This recipe places beets at the center of a salad, which will help detoxify the liver during recovery from alcohol, drugs, or pharmaceuticals.

Ingredients

3 cups spinach

2 cups arugula

1½ cup avocado, diced

½ cup cherry tomatoes, halved

¼ cup red onion, thinly sliced (optional)

2 tbs. lime juice

½ tbs. fresh jalapeno, seeded and minced

1½ tsp sea salt

1 cup cooked and sliced beets

Directions

- Combine all ingredients, except the beets, in a mixing bowl and mix well. Once tossed, add the beets to the top.

- Drizzle a little olive oil over the salad and add crumbled sheep feta cheese, if desired.

Less-Stress Sweet Vegetable and Meat Stew

This dish is ideal for when you want something nourishing and sweet to fill your belly to reduce stress and cravings. It is a one pot stew that requires a minimum of preparation. Because you are using inexpensive stew meat, organic, free range beef is affordable. This dish is indicated especially for someone coming off a sugar addiction or craving, as well as people in addiction recovery or whose digestion is weak. It is easily digested and there are a lot of nutrients in the juice.

Ingredients

2 lb. organic stew meat

3 medium carrots, sliced into ¼-inch coins

2 medium parsnips, sliced into ¼-inch coins

2 medium potatoes, sliced and quartered

4-5 cups water

2 bay leaves

½ cup mixed dried fruit* (prunes, pears, apricots, and/or apples), chopped into 1-inch pieces. Use organic fruit with no sulfites.

½ lemon, including peel, seeded and chopped into ½-inch pieces

½ orange, including peel, seeded and chopped into ½-inch pieces

¼ tsp. cinnamon

*Make sure you purchase dried fruits without preservatives, because the preservatives can alter mood and exacerbate asthma or breathing difficulties.

Directions

- Cut the meat and vegetables into 2-inch pieces and place in the slow cooker with 4 cups of water and the bay leaves. Cook for 2 hours on high (4 hours on low).

- Add the dried fruit and cook on low for an additional hour.

- Add lemon, orange, and cinnamon at the end. Stir well and let sit for 30 minutes.

- Serve in bowls.

Cooking Tip: While many people peel the skins off of vegetables, most vegetables should be cooked or eaten raw, with their skins on. Just use a vegetable brush to wash the vegetables well. The skin contains minerals and nutrients along with fiber for good digestion and balanced glucose uptake.

Sugar-Free Berry Sauce

Sometimes we have a hankering for something sweet or we want a healthy alternative to commercial fruit yogurts. This sauce makes a delightful topping on Greek yogurt or gluten-free pancakes. You can make it ahead of time and keep it in the refrigerator to satisfy your sweet tooth. This sauce can be enjoyed hot or cold.

Ingredients

4 cups (32 oz.) fresh or frozen berries of your choice (blackberries, blueberries, raspberries, strawberries, etc.)

⅓ cup water

⅓ tsp. stevia extract powder

4 tsp. arrowroot powder

⅓ cup water

Directions

- Add berries, water, and stevia to a medium saucepan. Bring to a boil, reduce heat and simmer 3 minutes.

- Dissolve arrowroot powder in the remaining ⅓ cup water and stir this mixture into the berries. Continue simmering another 2 minutes.

- Serve warm over muffins or gluten-free pancakes. Store leftovers in the refrigerator.

Healthy Happiness Brownies

Chocolate enhances mood, increasing energy and the neurotransmitter dopamine that helps us focus and be productive. Isn't that why we go for chocolate toward the end of our day as our energy lags? However, commercial chocolate is all too often mixed with sugar, which decreases our energy. We also crave chocolate because it is rich in magnesium which relaxes our mind as it relaxes our muscles. So the next time you want chocolate, don't feel guilty, but revel in the mood medicine this gluten-free recipe offers. Make it in double batches and freeze it in sections.

Ingredients

¼ cup rice flour

¼ cup tapioca flour

¼ cup chocolate powder

6 oz. chocolate (72% dark semisweet)

2 oz. chocolate (14% milk)

8 tbs. unsalted butter

½ tsp. baking powder

2 whole eggs, beaten

⅔ cup honey

4 drops liquid stevia

½ cup cooked oatmeal

⅔ cup almond flour

¼ tsp. sea salt

1 cup walnuts, chopped (set aside 20 whole nuts for garnish)

Directions

- Set out three bowls: One for melting chocolate (about 4-cup size), an 8-cup bowl for mixing the dry ingredients, and a 12-cup bowl for mixing the wet ingredients (and then combining with the dry ingredients).

- Break two large eggs into the wet bowl and whisk vigorously until nicely whipped.

- Combine stevia and honey (or agave) with the eggs until thickened and fully combined. Set aside.

- Combine rice flour, tapioca, and baking powder in the dry bowl and set aside.

- Bring a pot of water to a near boil, then turn the heat off. Place the chocolate bowl over the water (ensure the bottom of the bowl is not touching the water) to warm up.

- Chop the chocolate into about ⅛ inch or smaller pieces.

- Place in the bowl now seated on the water.

- Add the butter and the chocolate powder. Using a soft spatula, stir the combined chocolate and butter ingredients occasionally until fully melted, smooth, and glossy.

- Being careful to wipe the water from the warmed bowl of chocolate, pour the chocolate into the egg mixture, stirring as you do, and use the spatula to remove all of the chocolate.

- Stir while forming a light chocolate batter.

- Add the moistened oatmeal to the batter, stirring to combine. The rich, dark chocolate batter will now be a little lumpy, and thicker. That is good.

- Using a wooden spoon or spatula, stir in the dry ingredients, adding them in two batches.

- Stir in the chopped walnuts.

Preparing to Bake

- Preheat your oven to 350° F with the rack on the lowest level.

- Place parchment paper in an 8 x 8 x 2-inch glass or anodized cake pan, being sure to cover the walls to near the top.

- Garnish the top of the batter in the pan with 20 strategically placed nuts. (Hint: place a nut in each corner, then a nut in the middle between each corner nut, then fill in the empty spaces until you have a perfectly aligned nut pattern providing for 20 cut pieces of brownie.)

- Bake for 45 minutes, or until a knife comes out clean when inserted intothe middle. Do this test after 40–50 minutes.

Healthy Cocoa

Stress often underlies self-medication behaviors. It can also lead to high blood pressure. Cocoa is rich in polyphenols, which protect the endothelial lining of the arteries and reduces blood pressure. This increases blood and oxygen flow to the brain to support recovery. This drink is also a satisfying drink to use when eliminating sugary chocolate and candies from the diet. Be careful not to overdo the cocoa as it can be stimulating.

Ingredients

1 tbs. organic pure cocoa (no sugar added)

1-3 drops liquid stevia

1 cup fresh whole organic cream, or almond or rice milk

Directions

• Place the cream in a small saucepan. Add stevia and cocoa. Heat gently (do not boil) and have as a treat.

NOTE: Purchase a small handheld frother to froth the hot cocoa.

Liver Cleanse for Addiction Recovery

The Liver Flush is an ancient Ayurvedic drink and detoxification process that aids the liver. As the major detoxifying organ of the body, this flush helps the liver do its job more efficiently. It leads to more energy, improved sleep and is especially helpful when recovering from substance abuse. Do this process every 3 months (not more!) and notice the difference in your mental and physical well-being.

Ingredients

6 oz. fresh citrus juice (orange is ideal but it must be fresh, not carton or frozen)

1-2 slices of fresh ginger, minced

1 tbs. cold pressed olive oil

Directions

- Blend everything together until smooth and drink in the morning before breakfast with Polarity tea (see recipe in the Insomnia section).

10-Day Liver Cleansing Diet

Begin each morning with the Liver Flush and Polarity Tea (see recipe in the Insomnia section).

For the rest of the day, eat only fruits and vegetables (stay away from starchy vegetables like potatoes and squash). The vegetables can be consumed raw, steamed, or baked.

Olive oil, lemon, and garlic dressing may be used, but only after the vegetables have been cooked – do not cook in the oil!

Maintain this diet for 3-10 days. Headaches, nausea, and flatulence are a normal part of the cleansing process and should not be of great concern.

Take it easy during this cleansing period.

You may eat as many fruits and vegetables as you wish.

Culinary Herbs for Addictions

Ginger

An Old Indian Proverb says: *"Everything good is found in Ginger."* Ginger is a remarkable rhizome that can be used in a variety of ways to support addiction recovery.

Because most all addictions—alcohol, drugs, medications, food—negatively affect the liver and digestive process, ginger can help support liver and digestive function and aid in the absorption of nutrients needed for belly-brain-mind recovery. It is also stimulating, energizing, and refreshing at a time when withdrawal from any substance can lead to fatigue. Cook with ginger, add it to the Liver Cleanse Drink or simply boil it and make a tea to which you add a little lemon and honey.

1 thumb length sized piece of ginger cut into thin slices

4 cups of water

Add the ginger to boiling water and then simmer for 15 minutes until a golden yellow. Strain and add a little honey, or stevia, and lemon, if desired.

Peppermint

Peppermint aroma lifts mood and aids memory. The tea helps digestion and headache pain, and reduces gas and nausea. It is an ideal tea to drink after a rich meal or in the afternoon when you feel your energy start to drop. The scent is more important than the taste for altering brain function. Peppermint oil can also be dropped into some boiling water when you feel low, and it will quickly energize you and help you to focus.

Mint-Berry Cooler

Ingredients

8 oz. mineral water

4 oz. strong peppermint tea (cold)

3 tbs. fresh or frozen raspberries or blackberries

Ice to taste

Top with fresh peppermint
or spearmint

Directions

- Place the mineral water, lemon, berries, and ice in a large glass. Top with the fresh peppermint and serve.

Eat Right, Feel Right

Improve mood, sleep and focus with these nutrient-rich recipes & quick tips. *Eat Right, Feel Right* teaches you the do's and don'ts of using ingredients in entrees, snacks, soups, smoothies and dressings to make you an at-home mental health chef.

- Focus inducing capabilities of lemons and chocolate
- How to start a love affair with beets
- The anxiety reducing powers of vinegar
- How sweet potatoes support an immune system under stress
- Benefits of watermelon as a sleep aid
- Which foods to avoid
- And much more!

Leslie Korn, PhD, MPH, LMHC, specializes in mental health nutrition, somatic therapies and psychotherapy for PTSD, chronic illness and optimal cognition. She completed her clinical training at Harvard Medical School and her life training in the jungle of Mexico. She is the author of *Rhythms of Recovery: Trauma, Nature, and the Body, Nutrition Essentials for Mental Health* and *Multicultural Counseling Workbook*.

PESI Publishing & Media
www.pesipublishing.com